Redditch

on old picture postcards

Chris Jackson

1. A composite card of Redditch published by Valentine of Dundee, and posted in September 1957. All the composites I have seen feature St. Stephens Church in the centre. The other views here are (clockwise from top left): Evesham Street, showing the 'Hungry Man' public house and Evesham Street Post Office; the Parade, with the Redditch Benefit Building Society offices and a bus standing at the end of Church Road; the County High School in Easemore Road; and Feckenham Road at Headless Cross.

£2.95

Designed and Published by
Reflections of a Bygone Age,
Keyworth, Nottingham

ISBN 0 946245 85 1

Printed by
Adlard Print and Typesetting Services,
Ruddington, Notts.

St. Stephens Church, Redditch.

2. St. Stephen's Church on Church Green in the centre of Redditch is seen on a card posted to Upton-on-Severn in February 1908. *'"Thought you might like this one for your collection,"* wrote Ada.

INTRODUCTION

Having lived all my life in Redditch I have an understandable affection for the town. A keen interest in philately led eventually to my collecting Redditch postcards, not for the picture but for the cancellations. I soon realised that the picture side was much more interesting.

This book is a very small part of my collection of postcards of Redditch and the surrounding area. It is intended to show Redditch as it was earlier in this century; the cards range in date from 1902 to 1945. I hope older Redditch people will find it will promote memories of their lives in the town and that newer people will find it of interest in portraying how Redditch used to be.

Certain parts of the town have changed very little over the years but other parts have disappeared completely underneath the Kingfisher Shopping Centre and other "New Town" developments.

Redditch had a number of local photographers who produced cards in vast quantities. Most notable were A. Harold Clarke and F.A. Hodges who advertised *"local view cards a speciality"*, others included Lewis Brothers, L.L. Sealey, Joe Harman and many more. Several local postmasters published cards produced by national photographers. Probably the most prolific, though not the best quality, were those produced by Burrow of Cheltenham.

It is these people who we have to thank for producing these postcards which are, in many cases, the only pictorial records of the time.

Depending on the success of this book I hope to be able to produce further books on Redditch, *"Granny Locks to the Star & Garter"* and *"Gone Forever"*, based on the short talks I have given to local societies, are already being planned.

I have attempted to ensure the details contained in this book are correct; if I have made a mistake please forgive me, but let me know! I am always interested in obtaining more detailed information and expanding my collection. I can be contacted on (0527) 544722.

Chris Jackson
February 1994

Back cover (top): A composite by Jackson and Sons of Grimsby. The top left view is of the upper part of Evesham Street with the 'Fleece Inn', Brown's seedmerchants, and, in the distance, the Alcester Co-op. Card posted from Crabbs Cross in May 1914.

(bottom): Frith of Reigate published this card in the early 1950s. As well as the orthodox central view, it featured the Church gardens and fountain; the gardens of remembrance on Plymouth Road; St. Peter's Church, Ipsley, and the Parade. The card was sent from Park Road to Oswestry in October 1953.

3. A postcard view of the church from the top of Prospect Hill. The fountain was given to the town by the Bartleet family when the mains water supply was brought to the town in 1883. It depicts a female figure to represent temperance. Behind the fountain can be seen the town bandstand. This card was published by R.B. & E.D. Richards of Strensall, York.

4. The corner of Evesham Street and Market Place, with James Huins' boot and shoe shop prominent. Hodges' stationers was the next shop on Evesham Street, followed by Boots the chemist, Preedy's (tobacconists), a butcher's shop, and Brough's, gentleman's outfitters. Mrs. Fourts' hat shop was adjacent to Huins on Market Place. No indication of who published this card.

5. The entrance to Evesham Street, with Cranmore Simmons on the right. This was demolished and became first Burtons, then the present site of the Yorkshire Bank. Postcard published by H.W. Huckfield (no.952) and sent to Cheltenham in April 1921.

6. Evesham Street looking towards Church Green, with Humphries' shoe shop, one of only two shops off this old street which still exist in the Kingfisher Centre. Note the two eagles on the roof. On the left, behind the trees, was the congregational church with its needlemakers' graveyard.

RDH.54 EVESHAM STREET, REDDITCH

7. A card published by Francis Frith of Reigate in the 1960s, showing Evesham Street looking towards the traffic lights. On the extreme left is Worcester Road, with the 'Gaiety Cafe' and the 'Talbot Hotel' on the corners. On the right is Hollingtons, and on the corner of New Street is Hopkins, the jewellers.

CHURCH GREEN FROM PROSPECT HILL.

8. The top of Prospect Hill with a Midland Red single-decker bus outside the hospital. The enormous bag on the roof was to hold gas: petrol shortages during the First World War led to several bus companies converting their vehicles. The building on the end of the Green was the public toilets, removed when the underground toilets were built on the Parade. Postcard published by E.A. Hodges of 1 Evesham Street, and postally used in May 1919.

9. Card by A. Harold Clarke showing Church Green East. A super display of hardware is in evidence, including a child's chair, wooden rakes and a scythe. Other shops are Fogg's paper, tobacco and sweet emporium, the East Worcestershire Waterworks shop (which used to have a large gauge on the wall showing the pressure in the water main), Lloyds Bank, since refurbished to its original state, and Webb's cakeshop and bakehouse on the corner of Peakman Street. The postcard was sent from Redditch in August 1907.

10. The entrance to Redditch railway station at the bottom of Unicorn Hill. The large white house over the bridge is the vicarage. Wilkes' shop, later to become Biddles, was on the corner. All this has now been filled in; the bus station which now stands there is level with the bridge. Another card by A.H. Clarke, with the usual groups of children featured.

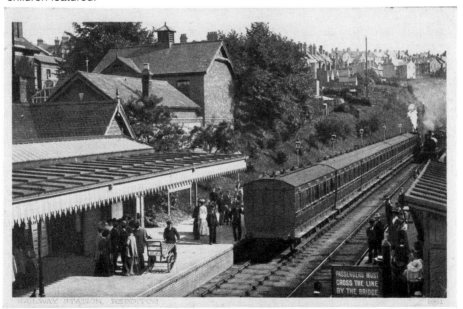

11. The Midland Railway came to Redditch in 1859, with the original station being built in Clive Road. Nine years later it was moved to the bottom of Unicorn Hill; the line was eventually extended through the tunnel under Mount Pleasant to Evesham. Redditch is now the end of the cross-city line. Postcard published by E.A. Hodges, and sent from Redditch in February 1912. The sender wrote *"This is not such a country village as the station leads one to suppose"*.

12. A formal picture of Redditch Charity Band with their trophies on display in 1933. Run by Mr. Wilkinson, it was extremely successful. I'm looking for assistance in identifying the people on this postcard published by Joe Harman – can you help?

13. The Charity Band on parade in Easemore Road, probably at a carnival. The man in the trilby hat in the foreground is believed to be Mr. Wilkinson; the building in the background was Frank Donald, printers. The Day Centre stands there now.

Market Place, Redditch

14. Market Place, showing the 'Royal Hotel' with Barclays Bank next door. Some of the upper bay windows above the shops still exist. Woolworths and Freeman Hardy & Willis are higher up the street, with Hepworth's Corner in the distance. Card posted to Bradford in October 1931.

Redditch, The parade.

15. The Parade, Redditch, featured on a Frith card postally used in July 1954. On the left is the very distinctive facade of the gas showrooms, now McDonalds. Buckley's tobacco and sweet shop is on the corner of William Street. The entrances to the underground toilets are visible behind the parked cars.

16. Market Place when it had a market. For many years the stalls backed onto the church railings. Hepworth's Corner at the top of Unicorn Hill is in the centre of this postcard in the "Huckfield" series (no.949) and McQuay's milliners is on the left.

ARKET PLACE, REDDITCH, No 949.

H W Huckfield's Series

17. The Parade on a 1950s Valentine postcard, with the picture taken from the fountain. The bus stands on the corner of Church Road, and behind it can be seen the offices of the Redditch Benefit Building Society. Cranmore Simmons is in the distance at the junction of Evesham Street and Unicorn Hill.

SMALLWOOD HOSPITAL, REDDITCH.

E. A. HODGES STATIONER, REDDITCH

18. Smallwood Hospital on a card published by Hodges about 1910. It was built by the Smallwood brothers, who were also responsible for building the almshouses in Mount Street.

19. The female ward of Smallwood Hospital on a 'pound card' for Saturday 23rd May 1914. The card invites donations of 'one or more' pounds in money or provisions. In return, donors were invited to inspect the hospital between 2 and 6.30 p.m.

18-35   BATES HILL METHODIST CHURCH, REDDITCH

20. The Methodist Church, opened in 1843 and extended in 1881, stood between Bates Hill and William Street. It was demolished in the early 1980s and is now the site of the Apollo electrical store. A Hodges postcard, sent to Kings Norton in December 1942.

21. St. Stephen's Church under repair in June 1905. Mr. Lewis, then the town librarian, is believed to be the brave man who took a plate camera to the very top and took four photographs, one from each direction. 89 years later, the church is currently fundraising again.

22. One of the views referred to in the previous caption: looking down Prospect Hill. The very high angle makes the aspect seem much flatter than it actually is. The fountain is visible in the foreground, and Easemore Road goes right from the centre. Beech House, for many years Whiteley and Pickering, is on the right.

23. Church Green East from Alcester Street with a saddler's shop on the right sporting a horse's head and travelling trunk above the door. It is now the site of the National Westminster Bank. Postcard in the "Lindley" series, posted to Crewe from Crabbs Cross in December 1905.

REDDITCH 7

24. The church of Our Lady of Mount Carmel in Beoley Road, built in 1834, and believed to be the first Catholic Church erected in England since the Reformation. It was not until the Catholic Relief Act of 1829 that building of churches was allowed to resume. The sender, having bought the postcard locally, posted it in London in December 1910.

25. Alcester Street from Market Place, showing the building on the end of Red Lion Street. Part of the advert for Watkins Tea Rooms on the wall to the left is still visible today. Lewis Brothers' photographers premises are on the right. This postcard, published by Hodges, was sent to Newport, Monmouthshire, in September 1908.

26. The lower part of Alcester Street with the 'Nags Head Inn' on the left. After Smith Street is Jock Jarvis's barber shop, the 'Rising Sun', and Steeles' butchers. The Baptist church is centre distance and the Mart auction rooms in the right foreground. In the middle distance, next door to the coach garage, is Fairest's model and toy shop. Card by A.M. Scriven of 45 Evesham Street.

27. The junction of Ipsley Street and Alcester Street, Poole Place. C.G. Huins, the builders on the corner were responsible for many local buildings, including the 'Palace Theatre' and the building society. Adjacent can be seen F. Williams the watchmaker and Shrimptons the draper. The 'Jubilee Oak' public house (later to become the 'Alma Tavern') is on the corner of Red Lion Street in the centre of the card, which was published in 1910. This scene is now the site of the Town Hall and the Ringway.

28. Bromsgrove Road looking away from the railway bridge c.1910. Edward Street is on the right. The large building was Hessin's needlemakers factory, which became Martinez and Bird.

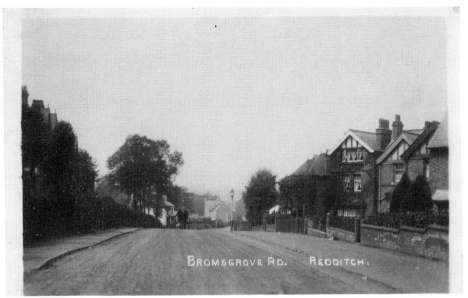

29. Bromsgrove Road from the top of the hill by the entrance to the Valley Stadium. The 'Queens Head' public house is left of centre, and the houses on the right are still standing. In September 1925 Nina wrote *"the town, although not large, is well-kept and pretty"*.

30. 'Holmwood', Redditch, was built by Canon Horace Newton as his private house in Woodland off Plymouth Road. It became a convalescent home for the Royal Antideluvian Order of Buffaloes. The cross on the second window from the left is to indicate the writer's room to the recipient in the message on the back. Card published by E.A. Hodges about 1918.

Holmwood. R.A.O.B. Reddhtch.

HART'S STUDIOS
WOLVERHAMPTON

31. Published by Hart's Studios, this card shows the interior of the lounge at Holmwood with the obligatory aspidistra and a gramophone on the table to the left. Hart's produced a large selection of cards of the house showing all the main rooms during the period when it was a convalescent home.

FOXLYDIATE VILLAGE NR. REDDITCH

32. Foxlydiate Village was a popular stopping-off point for cyclists: both the houses on the left and right advertise teas for them. In the centre is the 'Fox and Goose' public house, which was knocked down when the road was widened in 1938. The licence was transferred to the 'Foxlydiate Hotel' across the road when it was built later in the year.

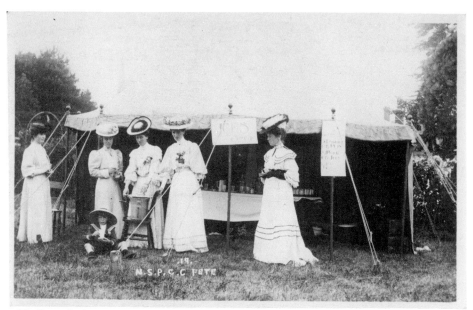

33. One of a large series of cards produced for the N.S.P.C.C. fete held in the grounds of Foxlydiate House in 1906. The house stood where the 'Foxlydiate Hotel' is now. The sign offers "ices", "a pastoral play" at 3 p.m. and 6.45 p.m., with Punch and Judy at 4.30 and 6.15, and a men's hat-trimming competition at 5 p.m.!

34. St. Stephens School, now part of the North-East Worcestershire College site, stood on the corner of Archer Road and Peakman Street. This card by Hodges was sent to Weston-super-Mare in August 1944 with the message *"Sorry, I couldn't find a card which is interesting. This is the best I could find."*

35. The County High School on Easemore Road, opened in the early 1930s. The headteacher's house is just off to the right of the picture. The sports facilities have improved somewhat over the years!

36. Evesham Road, Headless Cross, looking towards the town. On the left is the 'Dog and Pheasant' public house, and the distinctive skeleton spire of the Headless Cross Methodist Church, which was rebuilt after being blown down in 1895. On the right is Webster's Garage, now Knott's motorcycle shop. The message on the card refers to *"several air raid warnings".* It was posted to Leicester on 16th August 1940.

BIRCHFIELD ROAD, HEADLESS CROSS.

PUBLISHED BY ALFRED IRESON
STATIONER, HEADLESS CROSS

37. Nailpasser Green, at the junction of Birchfield and Rectory Roads, looking towards Feckenham Road. On the left is the 'Scale and Compass' pub, now 'The Archers'. This postcard was printed by Burrow of Cheltenham especially for Alfred Ireson, the postmaster at Headless Cross Post Office on Evesham Road. It was postally used in March 190**6.**

38. The visit to Redditch of Labour Party leader Keir Hardie was recorded by several photographers. He spoke for over one and a half hours and regaled local Labour supporters for not doing more to return a Labour M.P. Note the man on the right of the stage who is writing furiously – there is a word-by-word report in the following weekend's edition of the *Redditch Indicator.*

39. Redditch fair on a postcard sent to London in June 1908. *"Can you find anyone you know?"* asked the sender. Judging by the crowd, the helter-skelter was popular.

40. A school treat on 16th July 1910. It looks as if the whole town was out, with Evesham Street packed with people. E.A. Hodges' shop advertises commercial and fancy stationery, picture postcards, and an agency for Goss and Worcester china.

41. Webheath and district's flower show in 1908 being opened by Mrs. A. Eadie, wife of the founder of the Eadie Hub Company, which held the patents on a freewheel hub for bicycles and was the forerunner of the Enfield Cycle Company.

42. This was originally built in 1911 as the village hall for Tardebigge, but later became a recovery hospital for soldiers in the First World War, and more recently it has become a restaurant and bar. When it was built, it contained workrooms for the craftsmen employed at Hewell Grange. Card published by W. Terry, Victoria Studio, Redditch.

Hewell Hall, Redditch.

43. Hewell Hall about 1912. It took seven years to build (from 1884-91) and is reputed to have cost a quarter of a million pounds. Designed by Thomas Garner, it was planned as a vast renaissance palace modelled on Montacute Hall in Somerset. There is clearly Italian influence in much of the styling and fittings. The property is now a remand centre.

44. Milwards factory in Ipsley Street, built on the site of the 'Fountain Inn'. It will be remembered by many for its clock tower and the number it employed. The building existed until the late 1970s, but is now the site of do-it-yourself stores Wickes and Halfords. This card was posted at Redditch in May 1906.

45. The Holloway, home of the Milward family, was built on the ground between the 'Kings Arms' on the Holloway and Union Street, only yards from the factory. All that remains are some of the fine trees. It is shortly to become the Redditch Business Park.

THE LODGE POOL. NEAR REDDITCH.   PUBLISHED BY H. WILKES, REDDITCH

46. The Lodge Pool on Lodge Park. Despite recent notoriety for the bus station in Redditch as the world's most boring postcard, I can only assume no-one sent this card in! What a grey foreboding place this card, published about 1908 by H. Wilkes of Redditch, makes it look.

47. The farmhouse at Lodge Farm, a substantial family home, which was demolished when the Lodge Park Estate was built. Postcard published by A.W.S. about 1910.

48. Unicorn Hill about 1906, with the entrance to one of the infamous 'yards' in the right foreground. Daniels' newsagents and postcard seller is on the right and Bernard Wheeler's cake shop on the left. The large building in the centre became the 'Danilo' cinema. The cobbles were retained on the left of the road for many years, to give horses better grip when coming up the hill from the railway station.

49. The 'Kings Arms' at the junction of Beoley Road, The Holloway, Other Road and Ipsley Street. Mount Carmel Church is in the background. The 'Kings Arms' is now only two-thirds the width, having been rebuilt when the Holloway was widened. Postcard by L.L. Sealey of Beoley Road, posted to Derby in May 1911.

50. Hewell Road with its high-level access roadway which ran from Melen to Adelaide Streets. The lower part remains, but the part shown in this c.1925 view has disappeared under the Ringway.

SMALLWOOD ALMSHOUSES, REDDITCH.

51. The Smallwood Almshouses in Mount Street, built and endowed by William Smallwood out of money endowed to him by his brother Edwin. The buildings were opened for occupation on 22nd June 1897, Queen Victoria's Diamond Jubilee. Card posted in January 1904 to Virginia Water.

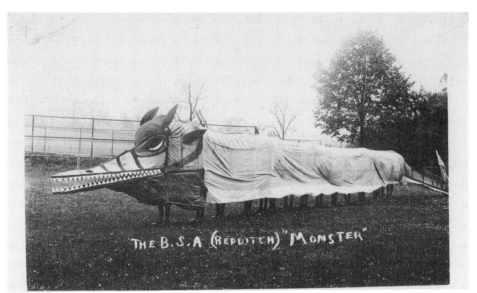

52. A dragon made by the B.S.A. Scouts for the jamboree in Perdiswell Park at Worcester. The scouts had alternate green and red socks, and the dragon breathed fire. The message on this 1920s postcard refers to 'dad' having shaken hands with chief scout Baden Powell.

53. The ford at Beoley Brook on Beoley Road on a card posted at Redditch in August 1920. This was a hazard on the main route to Birmingham before the main A441 was opened. It was well-known for strong currents and sudden flooding. The broken sign used to say *"not safe at 3 feet,"* but the lowest measurement on the post was 4 feet 6 inches!

MILWARD'S NEEDLES

I think the needles are excellent

28 · April 1906

Ellen Terry

54. An advertising card for Milwards needles. Ellen Terry was a leading actress of the Edwardian era, when many in her profession endorsed a variety of products. This postcard was sent from Hyde Park to Southfields in September 1906.

55. Ipsley Court, next to St. Peters Church at Ipsley. It is now the headquarters of the Law Society.

56. Oakley Road, Redditch, showing Ludlow Road going off to the right in the foreground. The shop seen here was until very recently an electrical store but is now a private house. The lower part of the road is under the bus lane of the Ringway. Card posted to Hull in September 1913.

57. The Mayfields is seen on a 1916 postcard, long before the estate was developed. The house in the foreground still exists, but the cottages were knocked down when the estate was built. The road appears to have been split even in 1916.

58. The aviator B.C. Hucks refuelling on the old racecourse at the bottom of Beoley Road. He was taking part in an air race with Gustav Hamel on 30th August 1913, sponsored by the *Birmingham Daily Post*. Hucks lost the race.